Dedication

My Love, my heart, my high school friend,
I've withstood the test with you until the end.
There's an ache in my heart living life without you here,
But still I trust in the Lord and know He's near.
Entertaining angels was all a part of the test.
I now realize that you are one of God's best.

I dedicate this testimonial to the memory of my beloved husband — **Justin Fefee**.

Acknowledgments

I would like to acknowledge the following:

My dad, **Andrew Davis**, for instilling in me the fear of God.

My mother, **Jacqueline Foster**, for being the invisible anchor in our lives (although she's never seen, she's there).

Andrea Davis, my sister, my better and other half, for being my voice when I couldn't speak, for standing when I couldn't stand and for holding me up when I could have fallen apart.

My pastor, **Mark A. Ellis,** for being the best pastor and leader on this side of Heaven.

My spiritual father, **Apostle Reginald Wilson**, for answering the call of God and guiding me through a stormy season in life.

The **participants** of the Command Your Day prayerline for praying and agreeing on my behalf for total freedom and victory.

Last but never least, my spiritual mother, **Terry Anderson Webb**, for covering me and holding me accountable, not allowing me to make excuses because of my circumstances.

I love you all and I truly appreciate all that you do.

God is my strength and power,
And He makes my way perfect.
2 Samuel 22:33, NKJV

Contents

Introduction 11

1. Childhood 15
2. A Deep Friendship 23
3. The New Man...............................31
4. For Better or for Worse 41
5. Closer to God 49
6. Bruised, but Not Yet Broken 55
7. My Calling 61
8. In Sickness and in Health.............67
9. Going through the Motions 79
10. Till Death Do Us Part 85
11. New Birth 101
    A Prayer of Salvation 106

Author Contact Information 107

*Life begins when you open up
your heart and receive the truth.
Until then, life is meaningless.*
— *Allison Davis*

Introduction

I had taken the children and gone to church alone that Sunday morning, leaving my husband of three years resting on the couch. The service was wonderful that day, and God did some very special things in my heart, even sending an angel to touch me. But now, as I approached the house on our way back home, I sensed that something was not right.

In that moment, the Holy Spirit spoke to me to leave the children in the car. I wasn't sure what this meant or why, but I knew what I felt, and so I didn't question God's Spirit. I calmly instructed the children to wait in the car for a minute, assuring them that I would be back for them soon. Then, a little tentative, I made my way inside to check on my husband.

I found him in exactly the same position he had been in when I had left that morning, but when I spoke to him, there was no response. His fingers were gray and cold, and so were his lips. It didn't take long for me to realize that my beloved husband had somehow passed away in my absence. My heart sank, and a whirlwind of emotions assailed me.

Strangely I felt no fear, and I felt no worry. I also didn't panic. But my heart did sink to the floor, and I was left standing there wondering how to deal with the situation.

One thought I remember was, "Oh my God, are you serious?" Another was, "Why today, Lord?"

Many other emotions began to overtake me in as what was happening began to become reality.

Who should I call? What should I say! And how should I say it? At the same time, all I could really say was, "Lord Jesus, please Help me!"

My first physical reaction was to resort to CPR and try to bring my husband back to life. I got him onto the floor and began to do chest compressions, but there was no response at all. A feeling of helplessness came over me as I realized that there was no life at all in his body.

But this was offset by the touch I had received from the angel at church. That angel seemed to be still with me, and a strange peace somehow overshadowed my sudden loss.

For what seemed like an eternity, my mind and emotions battled my spirit. Could it be possible? Could I be a widow at the tender age of twenty-eight? Could my beloved husband be gone after all we had been through and overcome together? What did all of this mean for the future of my children and for my own future? My heart was very heavy, but the Lord graced me with an unusual (and unreasonable) peace.

There were many questions I could not answer at that moment, but one thing I knew: the Holy Spirit had long been preparing me for this moment. It wasn't something I would have welcomed, but I knew that I would somehow survive it and go on to greater victories. After all, I had fought battle after battle and won them all. I had learned *The Power of a Hurting Wife.*

My prayer is that my testimony may strengthen many other women who are struggling with what life has thrown their way. May it restore their hope and save their marriages.

Allison Davis
Baton Rouge, Louisiana

Chapter 1

Childhood

For I know the plans and thoughts that I have for you,' says the LORD, 'plans for peace and well-being and not for disaster to give you a future and a hope. Jeremiah 29:11

My life has certainly not been a fairy tale, but it is most certainly my own story, and a very unique one at that. I would like to begin telling it when I was just three years old.

My parents were married and living together when I was born, but by the time I was three, they were separated and getting a divorce. I had an older sister, Andrea, and what I can remember from those days is that it was just the two of us. We did everything together (although Andrea mostly got into trouble on her own). I paid close attention to others' mistakes and tried to avoid them myself. (I wasn't always successful.)

Andrea and I had a very close bond. Oh, we had the normal sibling feuds from time to time, but nothing that could ever tear us apart. We were inseparable.

Our father had come to know Christ as a teenager, and by the time I was nine, he had introduced us to the Father, the Son, and the Holy Spirit. I can never forget that day, sitting in his Honda with my hands lifted, receiving the Holy Spirit into my life.

Dad remarried, and so did Mom. Because Mom was in an abusive marriage, Dad was the only one I felt I could turn to (seeing as though I was really too young to understand the power of God yet).

Dad and his new wife were soon expecting a baby (a boy), and they were so excited about that new baby that it made me feel very left out, almost unwanted at times. There was another reason I resented my dad. I often felt need of him, and he was never there to save me from the abuse I witnessed my mother going through. Little did I know that he was praying over us for our safety the whole time.

Calling on God was not yet a first response for me, but I was learning how to pray to Him when I was afraid. I do believe with all my heart that this kept my step-dad from hurting us.

Home was not a very happy place, so I found a friend in elementary school. Her name was April. I would go to April's house after class to avoid going home. This brought me a little comfort, but it was only temporary. April taught me how to be free in the mind and not worry about adult things. We played together for hours at a time, but then

I would eventually have to go home again.

Mom worked hard to provide for us, but it was very complicated for her to keep things consistently on the right track. There was a time when we were hungry and had no food in the house. I'm sure this must not have lasted longer than a day, but as small children that day felt like a very long time to us.

Soon we moved, and I lost contact with my friend April. In fact, we moved around so much during my childhood that I could never manage to keep friends for long. This caused me to find contentment within myself, and it also made me more aware of my surroundings. I still wasn't sure who the Lord was or how to live a Christ-like life. I saw the women in my life going through many difficult things, and I hoped to avoid them myself.

But then, at the tender age of thirteen, I was introduced one summer to sex. I think I knew in my mind that this was a sin, but no boy had ever spoken to me in the way this boy did, and I fell for it. I'm sure that I would not have wanted to do these things on my own, but I was still young and impressionable, and he convinced me to try it.

I felt horrible going into high school that fall knowing that I was possibly the only freshman who was sexually active. My parents had no clue that I was being seduced into this activity. Once I was in high school, I lost contact with the guy, and that was a relief.

It finally became clear to me that if I stayed at home, there is no way I could finish my studies. Mom was never home, and I needed academic support, someone to answer my questions when I had them and help me understand my lessons. I wanted very much to finish my studies, so I took the drastic step of moving in with my dad and step-mom.

A side benefit to this was that I was now able to go to church more. I was thankful for this opportunity. I wanted to know the Lord better, to worship Him and to stay away from sin. In my heart, I knew that it was time for a change. I had witnessed my sister becoming pregnant and giving birth at a very young age, and I had no desire to live that kind of life.

Being with Dad kept me involved with the church, and there I found a group of friends. While listening to God's Word and allowing Him to work in my heart, I began to understand that He still loved me and had a plan for my life. I remember sitting in a group class, learning and studying the Bible. I didn't quite understand everything, but I can still hear my dad saying "Pray for knowledge, wisdom, and understanding." It was sound advice, and that's what I did.

With everything, the ninth grade passed like a blur to me. Because I was living with Dad and my step-mom, I really felt quite alone. I noticed, however, that Dad was praying, and I sensed that this was the only thing that could really help me with my feelings of aloneness. So I increased my church attendance.

Now I went to cell group meetings and church revivals, and I also went to a retreat that changed my life. I knew that God loved me and that Jesus had given His life for me, but I did not fully understand ... until one night I went to the altar and someone told me that the Lord had forgiven me of the sin of fornication. This person knew nothing about me, so I knew the Lord had spoken to them. There was nothing quite like hearing from my heavenly Father direct for the first time.

Chapter 2

A Deep Friendship

*A cord of three strands is not quickly bro-
ken.*   Ecclesiastes 4:12

At the age of fourteen, I found my husband. His name was Justin Fefee. I was
only in the early years of high school,
but I knew the moment I laid eyes on
him that he was the one.

My best friend had introduced us the
summer before over the phone, and for
three months straight I had connected
with this boy I had not yet met physically. The two of us lived on opposite sides
of the city, and we were never meant

to be at the same high school, but suddenly there we were, in a ninth-grade math class together. This was where our journey together began.

We dated for a couple of weeks, but then we decided to just be good friends, and so all during our high school years, that's what we were—good friends.

He joked with me and said I was "mean and bossy." Despite the fact that he was now dating other girls, we remained very close. When I needed him, he was there for me, and when he needed me, I was there for him. I was sure that our bond was intended for much more eventually.

Strangely, we lost touch for about a year after graduation, and I was devastated. Every day I missed talking to him, and every day I wondered what it would be like to be married to him. What was worse, I wondered if I would ever see him again.

I had graduated, not knowing what exactly I wanted to do with my life, so

I decided to sit out college for the first year. During that year, I decided to go to beauty school, and that's what I did.

I was able to secure student loans to study cosmetology at the Aveda Institute here in Baton Rouge. I graduated two weeks early, took the state board exams and passed. I was now a licensed beautician, and with my degree in hand, I was able to work and earn. I worked at a daycare center during the week and a beauty salon on the weekends.

Through all of this time, I tried desperately to get Justin out of my mind by dating someone else. I dated one guy for three years and ended up getting pregnant by him. I was horrified by this turn of events.

"Oh, my goodness," I thought, "a baby." I cried for days, thinking about Justin and wondering if he had any children. I had no way of knowing.

When my daughter was born, I named her Ha'Ryon. Then, when she was only five months old, her father and I separated. It had been such a dangerous relationship that I was happy to be free of him. I was never actually physically abused, but the verbal abuse he dealt me was enough to keep me feeling as if no one would ever be happy in a relationship with me.

Now free from all that, I didn't waste any time searching for the man I knew had my heart—Justin Fefee. It took me about two weeks to find him.

I initially searched on the Internet, but when that failed, I finally called Justin's mom's house. He was there, but he was sleeping, I was told. I asked if someone could please wake him up. I needed to speak with him.

His step-father went to wake him and handed him the telephone. When I heard Justin's voice, my heart seemed to stop beating. I nearly cried, knowing that I had finally gotten hold of the man I loved.

A few minutes into the conversation I knew that I had to tell him about

Ha'Ryon. Not knowing how he would take the news, I yelled it out as if the words had jumped right out of my mouth. He laughed, but I could also hear the hurt in his voice. Within a few weeks, we were talking on a daily basis.

Eventually Justin said he would like to meet Ha'Ryon. I was worried about just how he would react to her, but I shouldn't have worried. When the two of them met, they instantly connected. From then on, he referred to her as his "little friend."

The drama with Ha'Ryon's real father was not over. Because I had decided to leave him, he was very bitter against me and began doing anything he could think of to hurt me. One day I was talking to Justin about this, and he suggested that it would be a good idea for me to move away from the area where we had been living. After talking about it for a while, he and I agreed to go in together and rent a condo. We would be roommates. I loved the idea.

I was blessed to be approved for the rental of a condo in nearby Denham Springs. Even though it was a bit over budget for me alone, I felt as if this would be okay. We had agreed to split the bills. This felt really good, a good friend offering to help me out with my bills. It was a means of finding a better life.

Since Justin and I were not in an intimate relationship, I felt as if it was all about me and my child. And things were going very well ... for about four months, and then "the new man" suddenly appeared.

God will sometimes allow us to go through things just so that we will desire Him more. He wants to be close to us, but He also wants us to want Him just as badly as He wants us.

Justin kept none of his promises to me, I ended up having to get a second job to make ends meet, and I lost our beautiful condo. That was a valuable lesson for me.

Some might ask, "Why in the world would you pay so much money for something you couldn't afford?" The answer is that I wanted it, and I prayed for it, so I expected God to provide for it. The problem was that I had a wrong motive. Just trying to prove a point to someone else was a bad idea. Often you hear people say, *"Be careful what you pray for"* (2 Peter 3:2). I learned my lesson through these prayers and, because of my bad decisions, I was to suffer a whole series of harsh lessons over the next five years.

Chapter 3

The New Man

"No weapon that is formed against you will succeed;
And every tongue that rises against you in judgment you will condemn.
This [peace, righteousness, security, and triumph over opposition] is the heritage of the servants of the LORD,
And this is their vindication from Me," says the LORD.   Isaiah 54:17

Who was this mysterious "new man"? When I decided to move and become roommates with Justin Fefee, I assumed that I was moving in with the same sweet, innocent, kind and do-no-wrong guy I had known throughout high school. How wrong I was!

During the months Justin and I had not been communicating, he had turned into an entirely different person. The things he was now involved with would never have occurred to me, and he now consistently ran with the wrong crowd.

After losing the condo, I was able to rent a small apartment, but our problems were not over. After being "just roommates" for those months, we had started dating, and now that I saw the other side of him, it was too late. I was already pregnant by him. This was a horrible situation. I now had a one-year-old child, a car that was on its last leg, two jobs to keep up with, was behind on all of my bills and was now expecting another child.

What this man was doing while I was at work I couldn't imagine. I can't say that he didn't help me at all, but the little he did help just wasn't enough. I was going to have to make a decision about this new baby I was carrying. I did love this man, and even through all that he had become and that was unfolding with us now, I still saw in him the boy I had fallen so deeply in love with in high school. But, I began to realize, he just wasn't ready for a baby. And, at the moment, I didn't feel capable of caring for a second child either.

At six weeks of pregnancy, I made the fateful decision to have an abortion. I was, for all intents and purposes, alone, and I couldn't care for two children and work at the same time. For the moment, I had to push God aside and do what my natural mind was telling me was right.

Of course, it was a mistake, by far the worst mistake I had ever made, and I have always wished I could take it back. I immediately knew it was a mistake, and I prayed and asked God for His for-giveness. But I could not allow this bad decision to cripple me. Somehow I had to move on with my life, and I could not go about that feeling crippled by guilt. I had heard horror stories of women who continued to have nightmares years after they had aborted a pregnancy. I needed God's help.

Soon after I had the procedure done, I lost my car in a vehicle accident and there was no way possible for me to get another one. I now had to depend on Justin to take me to work and to take Ha'Ryon to daycare. This worked well for a while, but then I had to make another big decision. Since I could no longer afford the condo, I needed to move.

I found an apartment, which was much less expensive, and I also decided to pull Ha'Ryon out of daycare to save more. I figured that since Justin didn't have a job at the time, he could keep her for me.

By this time, we had agreed to date again, and he took care of Ha'Ryon, as if she were his own. I never had to worry about him mistreating her. I trusted him. She was toilet trained before the age of two, and I can honestly say that I didn't have much to do with that. Justin was great with her.

But leaving Ha'Ryon at home with my boyfriend didn't last even a full year. I learned that sometimes he would leave her with someone else, while he did whatever he had to do. He made sure she had what she needed, but then one day, while I was at work, I received a phone call from someone telling me to come home and get my daughter before she was taken by child protective services. I panicked and thought "Oh, my goodness! What's happened to my child?" If something bad had happened to her, how would I tell her dad, whom I hadn't spoken to for years?

My questions were quickly answered. As I walked through the door of my apartment, I found a policeman holding my child, and there were about seven or eight other officers spread

out through my living room and bed-
rooms. They had destroyed the place
and left the mess for me to clean up.

As it turned out, Justin had allowed a
friend to bring a stolen gun and hide it
in our house. I had no idea it was there.
Now, because he had facilitated the act,
he was taken to jail.

It was a terrible moment. I was truly
disappointed in Justin, but I was also
frightened for him, and I was worried
that I was going to lose my job because
I now had no baby-sitter. I had to appeal
to members of my family to help me
with Ha'Ryon's care.

Justin served about three months away
from us, and then he was released and
came home. It was a very confusing time
for both of us. I had missed him and was
happy to have him back. Things could
now return to normal, and he could keep
Ha'Ryon while I worked. But the change
went deeper than that.

Justin truly seemed to be a changed
man, and he seemed to love and appre-

ciate us more now. We seemed to have turned a corner. In fact, he was doing so much better that we began to discuss having another baby.

This seemed to be very important to Justin, so I agreed. If things were getting better, why not have another baby? But, then, when I was just six months pregnant with this child, Justin made another bad decision, this time drug distribution, and it caused him to have to go away again.

Now I was completely aggravated. I had thought that this cycle of craziness was over. I had never been through so much in my life and wanted to give up. Still, the Lord was telling me to be strong and stop trying to control everything. He would help me — if I let Him do it.

But things were hard. Once again, I had no one to keep Ha'Ryon while I worked, and our bills were mounting and getting past due. I had to give up the apartment, and this time I had to move in with Justin's mom. At least I was comfortable, and they treated me very well, but there's truly nothing like having your own home.

Ha'Ryon stayed with my sister Andrea during the week while I worked. During the months in which I was waiting for the baby to be born, I was working and saving money so that we could move. From January through early March, I was there at Justin's mom's home. On March 3, I went to the hospital. As it happened, that very day Justin was released and joined me at the hospital in time to celebrate the birth of our son Judah. I named him Judah because the name meant praise, and I had needed to offer praise to God all the way through this ordeal.

Soon we moved out of Justin's mom's house into a small and affordable apartment. I worked really hard to get it, only to be told by the landlord that because of Justin's conviction, he couldn't stay there. He stayed anyway, and of course that caused a lot of issues with the landlord.

Aside from this, Justin and I were getting along very well. We did the family thing, and he was being totally responsible. He now agreed to keep both of the children while I was at work, and I was thinking, "What a great dad!"

Before long, however, I began to suspect that there was another woman. I couldn't put my finger on anything specific, so I had to let those feelings go for the time being. For a while, we lived a life that I can only call "okay."

Almost a year and six months after our son Judah was born, Justin and I got married. I knew in my heart that this man was my husband because I had a love for him like no other. I prayed and asked God about marrying him, and honestly the Lord told me that it wasn't the right time. Once again, however, I pushed the Lord aside and proceeded to do what I wanted to do. I believed that if I got married and stopped living in sin (shacking up) with Justin, then God would surely bless our relationship more.

One thing that I must say here is this: when you move outside of God's timing, you have to deal with the consequences of whatever decision you have made. If you trust God and allow the Holy Spirit to guide you, then, of course, He will.

Chapter 4

For Better or for Worse

For this reason a man shall leave his father and his mother, and shall be joined to his wife; and they shall become one flesh.

Genesis 2:24

Our legal marriage got off to a very rocky start. Only two weeks into our honeymoon stage, I learned that Justin had a newborn baby by another woman. I thought, "Man, what am I going to do? This is horrible."

I tried to talk to others about this, but I found no relief. I can remember just wanting to take my kids and run. I could not get past wanting to vomit. If you know anything about timing, then you know what I mean when I say God's timing is everything. I truly believe that I may have gotten married outside of God's timing. This marriage was nothing like I had thought it would be, and I then knew that I should have waited on the Lord. The hurt, pain, and shame were getting to me.

Depression began to sink in, and I was unable to think of anything else. I quickly realized that if I didn't get hold of myself, I was going to have a nervous breakdown. I prayed and asked the Lord to help me get over Justin's infidelity.

If I was going to be blessed, I had to let it all go and this letting-go process is never easy. All I can say is just give it to God, and He will take good care of you.

I admit that there were days when I did think about what Justin had done, and it would start to churn something up deep inside of me. In those moments I had to ask myself if I really wanted my marriage to work. If I continued to hold on to this hurt, there was no way it could survive.

There were times where I did not want to have sex with my husband because of what he had done, and of course, this was damaging to our marriage. I had to get over all of this, and I did.

Learning the power of forgiveness was very complicated, but knowing that the power of God could change things, I decided to give it a try. And suddenly, we were off to another good start. I cooked our meals, I cleaned our house, I worked and still took care of the family like a wife should. We were moving forward. After about six months of this, we were able to put the kids back in daycare.

Then it all came crashing down again. It wasn't long before I learned that Justin was living a double life. When I would come home from work in the evenings, he would take the car and leave, and I would be left alone with the children. Another woman had his attention now.

Once again I sought the Lord, this time on my knees. I asked Him for comfort, for strength, and for wisdom to do whatever I would have to do. I spoke to Justin about a dream the Lord had given me about him walking out on me. He denied that there was another woman, but two weeks later he left us.

Left with all of the bills and not enough income, I now tried my best to make life work for us. This time I resorted to fasting and prayer. I used it as a comfort and also to get closer to the Lord. In this situation, I desperately needed the Lord. The Bible shows us the many benefits of fasting and praying (see, for example, Joel 2:12).

I went through days of crying, feeling hurt and wishing I could be hit by a bus. That's how hard things were for me. The enemy was using my situation to try to pull me into a deep state of depression. I fasted and prayed for twenty-eight days straight.

When I ended the fasting, I weighed only ninety-eight pounds, but I didn't care what anyone said about it. I was on a mission.

The Lord spoke to me and promised that He would restore my marriage. I had never given up on Justin. The lady he was seeing was proud to try to ruin our family, and I was experiencing true spiritual warfare.

At first, I felt hopeless and helpless, but when I realized that it was the enemy who was attempting to destroy the unity Justin and I had enjoyed, I knew I had to fight for him. I trusted the Lord and stood on His Word.

What a hard time I had trying to do this! Emotionally I felt like I didn't want to ever love my husband again He had treated me as if I meant nothing to him. But I knew this was only the enemy attacking his mind. The Lord was calling me to love my husband anyway.

Then the love that I had for him was transformed into something totally different. I call it "a love without reason." Suddenly I loved him to the point that I went after him. He asked me, time and time again, for a divorce, but the Lord had other plans, so I kept telling him no.

He wanted to know why I was chasing after him. I wondered myself. I realize now that the Lord had me on a mission for the man's soul. What a powerful and merciful God, to meet us right in the middle of our mess and say, "Hey, I still love you, and I love you enough to come after you."

I desperately held on to what I knew was God's will. I had to hold on, for things got worse. Justin lost his job and ended up in a halfway house two hours away from us.

Now, it seemed, the Lord was pulling the rug out from under me. Everything that I had begun to do for myself, the Lord wanted to do for me. I surrendered fully and allowed Him to work on my behalf.

In the process of all this, I had to move out of my own place and back home with my mother. This, for me, was stressful. Never in a million years had I thought about going back home. Not that this was completely horrible, but home just wasn't comfortable for me anymore.

I begin to ask God to do His will in my life, but I also wanted my family back. You have to understand: my little family was what I had centered my life around. Working, feeding and caring for my husband and children, while putting God first ... that was my life. Now, however, life as I knew it had sort of flipped upside-down.

After spending time apart, Justin and I developed a different kind of relationship. Soon we were back on good terms again.

Now things at home took a turn for the worse. Mom lost her house, and suddenly the children and I were from one house to another, and this went on for three months. I finally found us a small house to live in. Again, there's nothing quite like having your own space.

Chapter 5

Closer to God

*Then [with a deep longing] you will seek Me
and require Me [as a vital necessity] and
[you will] find Me when you search for Me
with all your heart.* Jeremiah 29:13

There's something that happens when
you discover the power that God has
given to you. I became really excited
when I was told that God gives us au-
thority over the enemy so that we may
overcome the obstacles we face in life.

Soon after I found the house, Justin
was released from the halfway house,
and we were united as a family again.

I tried my best to trust him, but the infidelity had taken a lot out of me. The love that I'd had for him in the beginning stages had changed. I loved him stronger spiritually now, but I could no longer look at him in the same way.

Still, we went on, day by day trying to make our marriage work. But due to the spiritual discipline I had developed while he was in the halfway house, I knew that we could not make it without putting God first.

During the many trials that I faced in the early stages of our marriage, the only choice I had was to draw closer to God. I came to realize that the Lord had allowed me to go through many things so that my faith would grow stronger.

Even after I had overcome the infidelity, there were still numerous trials to face. I would never have imagined life as it was. When we tried counseling at our local church, many more of Justin's infidelities were revealed. After just one of those meetings, he never wanted to go back. How could we continue to get help for our marriage?

I can say to all who are married: never think that you don't need help, and never try to fix things on your own. Since you are married, you are no longer two. The two are now made one, so you should try to think as one and not for yourself individually. Agree to get help and move forward, striving for God's best for all concerned.

You should seek godly counsel and wisdom for help with all issues in your relationship. God sends us help for a purpose, and no one person has all of the answers.

Another key is to surround yourself with godly married couples and then observe them. Watch how the Lord has joined them together and how He uses them for His Kingdom.

Justin and I were not just on different pages; we were in two very different books. I have heard some people say, "We need to get on the same page."

Well, we were not even close to being on the same page. We looked at life very differently.

I had thought that after our separation, we would then come together stronger than ever, but, unfortunately, that didn't seem to be the case.

Once I saw that we could not agree on a certain way of living and knew that Justin would do what he wanted to do, I realized that I had to do what was right for me and for the children. I clung to the Lord and held on to His Word, determined to walk in His ways. But living in a home divided was very difficult.

As I was reading my Bible one day, I came across a scripture that spoke about a divided home not being able to stand (see Matthew 12:25). Still, the Lord shielded me and protected me from the things that were in the pit I found myself in.

Yes, it was a pit. I felt as if I was a child of God who had made some wrong decisions that had caused me to be thrown into a snake pit. I felt as if I was working hard just to keep going forward and trying my best not to give up.

There were also times when, after I had finished my daily routine, I felt as though I had been beaten and robbed of all my joy. Once again I pushed my way to the House of God to hear His Word.

When I didn't have strength to pray for myself, I would seek help from men and women of God. One day, a message entitled Brokenness was delivered in the church I was attending. At first, I didn't understand the message, but as I prayed about it, the Holy Spirit began to reveal the meaning of it to me.

Sometimes we get beaten up by life, but we can still push forward. We may even get knocked down at times. The thrust of the message was that we never get fully delivered from something until we have been broken. God has to break us away from some things or some people in order for Him to begin a mighty work in our lives.

We must never be too prideful to be broken. Allow God to pull some things out of you and heal you from your brokenness. That's what He did for me.

Chapter 6

Bruised, but Not Yet Broken

When you pass through the waters, I will be with you;
And through the rivers, they will not over-whelm you.
When you walk through fire, you will not be scorched,
Nor will the flame burn you.   Isaiah 43:2

To be so young still, what a life I have lived! I am convinced that my ancestors had prayed for me, and because of this, I developed a great amount of wisdom at an early age. There's nothing like having the Lord and His wisdom on your side.

Sometimes the enemy feels that if he can hurt you badly enough, you will harbor such great anger that it will paralyze your spiritual growth. You cannot grow when you hold anger, bitterness and resentment deep in your heart. I was determined to never allow the hurt and pain of betrayal to stunt my growth. Instead, I chose to let those things go. I had many bruises, but I was not yet broken. I chose life, and I chose to have it more abundantly. I refused to allow the circumstance of life to turn me into something or someone I did not enjoy being.

After years of pain and hurt, I honestly believed that things could not get any worse, but I was wrong. Now God was dealing with me in a way He never had before, and things got crazy.

My relationship with God was heading to a much deeper place, and this meant that in the natural all Hell was about to break loose. Just when I thought our life was taking on a more mature nature, here came the same situation again. The man who had vowed never to commit adultery had done it again. This brought all the past hurts flooding back.

It is quite possible to forgive someone but never forget, and that was what I had done. I had forgiven, but I had not forgotten the hurt and pain it had all caused me. Now it all came surging back again.

For the longest time, I struggled to know what I was doing wrong to make Justin do these things. Then, I realized that it wasn't anything I was doing. He confessed as much, saying that he just wanted to see if he still had what it took to get another woman. In my book, it was not an acceptable excuse, and it never would be, but at least now I knew.

I talked to Justin seriously, letting him know that if he couldn't get some counseling and get himself straightened out, then I intended to leave him. He began communicating with me more, and I began communicating with the Lord more.

I spoke with God about everything, and He sent me wise counsel. He sent me women who had been married for more than twenty years to instruct me and help me to see how to be better and do better.

In the face of the mistrust that had built up early in our marriage, I didn't give up hope, but I stopped chasing my husband. My attention now was on perfecting my walk with Christ, caring for my children and furthering my career.

Justin now came and went as he pleased, sometimes not coming home for days at a time. Of course I wondered where he was, but I remained focused on the children and my work.

I was still being guided by the Holy Spirit, and I prayed for Justin and lifted him up before the Lord.

One of the women God had sent to me instructed me about what to do when Justin came home late. When he came home at four o'clock one morning, I asked if he was okay and if he was hungry, and I treated him like a wife should treat her spouse. I was happy to see that he was well and alive. Although I was hurt and angry inside, I still approached him humbly and lovingly.

Never treat your spouse as if they are beneath you. Instead, always treat them as if you are serving Christ Himself. Do everything for them in love and kindness. Even when you are upset at their actions, you should strive to please the Lord with your own excellency, by being the best spouse you can be.

Whatever you do, don't look at what the other person isn't doing because if you do, God will judge you about your own actions. So even if that spouse is unfaithful and doesn't come home at night, give it to God and humble yourself, put a smile on your face, and let God get the glory out of your reaction to a painful situation.

Chapter 7

My Calling

*And let us not lose heart and grow weary
and faint in acting nobly and doing right,
for in due time and at the appointed season
we shall reap, if we do not loosen or relax
our courage and faint.* Galatians 6:9

More and more, my life was revolving around Christ, and I really pushed toward living a Christ-like life, devoted and dedicated to finding my true purpose in life. I had never been so close to the Lord before, and I begin to hear the voice of God clearly. To me, it was the same as if it had been audible. I have come to believe that our first test from God is in our ability to hear Him.

Now the Lord became my Best Friend because I couldn't tell my husband certain things or talk to him on a spiritual level. I didn't want to push him away from the Lord by going on and on, because he saw things differently than I did.

God also began to reveal things to me through dreams and visions. When I say this, I am not referring to any witchcraft or demonic activity. The Lord will show us things in order to prepare us for what is ahead, and also so that we can intercede for others.

The first thing the Lord revealed to me was my calling. I came to understand that I was called to intercede (pray deeply and consistently for) others. The Lord would place someone on my heart, and I would pray for them until I felt a release in my spirit. I also began to realize that, as a wife, I was on an assignment from the Lord, and my husband was my assignment.

I understood that I had been placed in Justin's life to cover him in prayer, and I did this with faith. As you have already seen, his life as a man was hard, but now things became even harder. While he struggled to make the right decisions, the Lord allowed me to watch him face battles that he tried to fight on his own. I watched him walk right into a brick wall of trouble, after I had warned him about it. It was so hard for me to just stand back and watch, knowing that his decisions were causing him such heartache.

But I had to realize that I could not change him. The only thing I could possibly do was to pray to the heavenly Father to change his thought processes and turn his hearts toward Him. This one realization saved me from an untold amount of worry and stress. Now, knowing what I had been placed here on earth to do, I had to get to work.

Suddenly I felt a burning desire in my heart to spiritually help others. Needless to say, Justin was heavy on my heart, and I desired to see him live well and happy. I began to notice that he, too, had a heart for others and the thought came to me: what a powerful couple we could be working together in the Kingdom of God! But, once again, I had to remember that I could not make someone do what I wanted them to do. I had a strong faith, however, that Justin would surely become the man he was called to be.

I prayed and asked God to help me see my husband through His eyes. He answered that prayer immediately, and I began to see so much more in Justin than I had before. Nothing he had done or would do could now make me look at or treat him as anything less than my husband and God's child, worthy of my love and respect.

I grew stronger and closer to God, and part of that was finding and joining a church that had a life-changing touch of God on it. I began going on spiritual retreats and meetings where there were other godly women. These women were married, and they were filled with the Holy Spirit, so they understood where I was coming from. Their counsel was invaluable and this allowed me to go deeper into my calling.

During this time, the Lord touched me in such a way that I wanted my children to know Him as well. I got them involved and active in the church, and they loved it.

I still wanted to have my house in order, and that meant having my husband saved and in church, but I knew that I had to go before the Lord for guidance in this. The more I talked about the Lord and modeled a Christ-like lifestyle, the more Justin seemed to push back against it. He wanted to live his life the way he wanted to live it. I knew that this was a very dangerous way of thinking, so I began to pray over his mind. I prayed that God would renew his mind and open his heart to receive Christ.

When you are constantly praying on behalf of someone else, you cannot afford to *"grow weary,"* as the Bible says in Galatians 6:9.

We must resist the temptation to turn from doing good because we feel as if our prayers are not being answered quick enough. God has equipped us to be able to withstand any storm or test in life—when we choose Him first. I chose to stand on this promise, no matter what, because I knew that in due season I would see those prayers being answered.

Chapter 8

In Sickness and in Health

And behold, the LORD passed by, and a great and strong wind tore into the mountains and broke the rocks in pieces before the LORD, but the LORD was not in the wind; and after the wind an earthquake, but the LORD was not in the earthquake; and after the earthquake a fire, but the LORD was not in the fire; and after the fire a still small voice.   1 Kings 19:11-12, NKJV

Standing on God's Word is what I learned to do best. Trials and test only made me turn to His Word even more often, because I knew that any test could be passed with His help. Through it all I grew even closer to God, and He began giving me vision after vision, preparing me for things to come.

One night at bedtime, I went around the house turning out the lights, and I stopped in to check on the children. Judah was at the foot of the bed turned sideways. Ha'Ryon was at the head of the bed curled up, and the comforter was hanging off the side of the bed. They looked fine to me, so I went on to bed.

While Justin and I were asleep, I had a dream about my deceased grandmother, and I woke up in tears. This woke Justin up too. Assured that I was okay, he proceeded to the rest room. When he returned, he got back in bed and went back to sleep.

But I couldn't sleep. The Holy Spirit began to speak to me in a small voice, as in the book of First Kings. But as still and small as that voice was, it had overtaken the room, and I could hear the Lord asking me if I trusted Him. I responded with a resounding yes.

He then asked me again and then again. I responded, "Yes, Lord, I trust You."

He then said, "Go check on the children."

I asked Justin if he had gone to check on them, and he said no. So I obeyed the voice of God and went to check.

The children were no longer in the positions they had been in when I had first checked on them. They were both at the head of the bed. I was stunned by this and also by the fact that they seemed to be all tucked in.

I went back to my room, but I didn't get back in bed. Instead, I sat on the edge of the bed, and the Holy spirit began to speak to me. He was telling me to trust Him with everything, even the children.

After having the Holy Spirit pay me a divine visitation that night, I never let that go. I prepared my house daily as if He were coming again that very day. I made sure I had the house cleaned and the family all comfortable before I would lie down. Justin often had different people coming in and out of the house, so I would go back and ask the Lord to bless our home and free it from any impurities.

Justin never fully understood this habit of mine, until I explained it to him one day. But he would still have his worldly company over, and these people were not good influences.

My children watched as I modeled how a real woman of God should live on a daily basis. I watched what I did and what I said around them, because I didn't want them confused. I am not perfect, and have had many flaws, but when it comes to training up my children, I know that I have to be careful as to what example I set before them.

Next God gave me a vision that something quite heartbreaking was about to happen. In this vision, God put me clearly in the middle of the situation, so that I could see exactly what would happen. I saw my husband being shot at. The Lord then told me, "He'll be okay." I was shocked by this and began to pray a hedge of protection over Justin and over that incident.

Then one day Justin and I had a serious talk about the power of making right decisions. Soon afterward, he went out, giving me an agreed-upon time that he would come back. I went to sleep before that time, but the Holy Spirit woke me up and said, "Get up and call your husband."

I called him and asked if he was on his way home yet. He replied, "No! In fact, I'm in a high-speed chase with about thirty police coming behind, and the driver won't stop to let me out." I knew that if the driver didn't stop, the police would eventually open fire on them. I thought back on the vision I'd had earlier, and I panicked.

I asked Justin what he wanted me to do, and he asked if I could pray and then call his mom. Then we were dis-connected.

I was so nervous that I couldn't pray, so I called my sister Andrea. She began to pray like I had never heard her pray before. Out of her heart poured a prayer that I am convinced saved my husband's life.

I then called Justin's mom to let her know what I knew. Justin had had a chance to tell me their location before we were disconnected, but after that I heard nothing more from him.

I turned on the local news and watched to see if there was anything on this inci-dent. I called around to nearby prisons to see if he might have been there, and his mom searched hospitals near the location he had given me.

After five hours of searching, she found Justin. He was in the hospital, but we were told we could not see him. He was in police custody.

It was four days before we were able to get any more information. What we then learned was that Justin was still alive, but had been shot three times. One lung had collapsed, and one leg had been broken. Just to know that God had kept His word, and my husband was "okay" brought tears to my eyes. What a mighty God He is to do what He said He would do in that situation!

But suddenly I realized that our lives had changed drastically overnight. Nothing would ever be the same again. Because Justin had a broken leg and a lung that was not functioning right, I would now have to care for him. He had lots of family members wanting to come over and help, but I felt that as his wife (and because I had made a vow before the Lord to love him in sickness and in health), I needed to be the one to care for him. I now bathed him, cared for his wounds and waited on him hand and foot. Never in a million years could I have imagined having to care for my husband in this way, but I knew that was what God wanted me to do, so that is what I did.

In spite of the fact that Justin had not taken my advice and had made another bad decision, I had to do what pleased the Lord. I never once complained about having to wait on him hand and foot because I didn't want anyone else taking care of him.

It was also my job during this time to cover Justin spiritually from every attack of the enemy. I never made him feel as if he were anything less than a man and a beloved child of God. Every time the Lord released me to give him a word, I did just that, but I also comforted him and encouraged him to keep his head up and look to the Lord and not to let his situation get the best of him.

As a result of his running from Christ and trying to live life through his own understanding, the Lord had been forced to stop him in his tracks and demand his full attention. While it hurt me to see him go through all that, I just prayed that he would understand the purpose behind it all. And, sure enough, he grew to understand spiritually what had taken place.

I was so grateful that Justin now understood what God wanted to do with his life. But, although he understood, it was obvious that he got a little weary while waiting on God.

About this time, I met my spiritual father, Apostle Reginald Wilson. The Lord sent him on assignment to come after me in the Spirit. From my understanding, he did not question God, and, instead, did just as he was told to do.

I had never experienced having a spiritual covering like this, so I did not know how to appreciate what the Lord was doing for me. Although I did not understand what exactly the Lord was doing in my life through the Apostle, I learned to surrender and trust God in this situation as well.

The Holy Spirit had spoken to me and said, "I want to do a new thing in you—if you will just allow Me to." I did not want to miss out on what God had in store for me. Once I surrendered to the voice of God and accepted what He wanted to do for me, He began working.

I began praying even more and prophesying over my home and my marriage that the devil would not win the battle because God had already won it.

From a wheelchair, to a walker and then to crutches—all within a matter of weeks—Justin was determined to regain his strength and walk again. Only three months after having his leg broken in half, he was back walking. I could not help but praise God and pray that Justin would now choose to walk with Christ, after all he had gone through.

But I had never witnessed anyone as strong willed as this man. He knew who God was and why he had suffered to learn it, and yet he still wanted to live his life the way he saw fit. I was terrified to let him go places with his different friends, but, once again, I had to remember that I could not control other people or manipulate them into doing what I wanted them to do.

As much as I hated it, I had to let Justin go where he wanted. The Lord told me to take my eyes off of my husband and to focus, instead, on Christ. He surely saw my tears and heard my cry.

Chapter 9

Just Going through the Motions

Therefore, put on the complete armor of God, so that you will be able to [successfully] resist and stand your ground in the evil day [of danger], and having done everything [that the crisis demands], to stand firm [in your place, fully prepared, immovable, victorious]. Ephesians 6:13

My marriage was now held up only by the arms of Christ. If it had been by my own will, I would have left the situation prematurely. During this time, it felt as if we were just going through the motions. Justin and I were living in the same house and trying to get along, but things were crazy. It really seemed as if our spirits were at war with each other.

I had my daily routine. Apostle Reginald had developed a group of believers who prayed together every morning by phone. He called it Command Your Day, and I loved joining them in prayer. After that, I had to get the children off to school, and then I had to get myself to work. My focus was caring for my children, growing my business and getting closer to God.

One thing is for certain: you can never be too close to God. I wanted to get even closer to Him. I certainly didn't want to just be going through the motions in my relationship with Christ. My marriage was another matter.

I began to notice different spirits that Justin's lifestyle attracted. Some of them were: thieves, liars, manipulators, spirits of drunkenness, spirits of drug addiction, and many others. Once I began to spiritually see these things, I sought the help of those on the daily prayerline, and they assisted me spiritually with anything and everything I needed. I was praying more and more for my family, and I began to feel Gods wonder-working power even more in my life.

I remember Apostle praying for me one day and asking God to open my eyes and give me a supernatural vision so that I might see through spiritual eyes. The result was that the Lord allowed me to see and understand how Justin was being attacked by the enemy.

At times, Justin was extremely generous and would give anything he had to meet the needs of others. What he didn't realize was that his friends were taking advantage of his generosity. At the end of every day, he would have nothing left, because he had given it all away (his money, his clothes and even his shoes).

I want to address married people who are just going through the motions, you know, the kind who say they are married (and legally they are), but their marriage is not working. Please ask yourselves these questions: Is God pleased with your marriage? What might your marriage have to offer in the way of advice to a newly wedded couple? Would you, as a wife or husband, separately be able to counsel that couple because you feel as if you individually have it all together?

Honestly, I believe that if you cannot bond together with your spouse, to help someone else who needs your help, then you may be the one who needs help. Although my marriage played out very different from what I am saying, through it I allowed Holy Spirit to teach me, shape me and mold me into a wife who was humble enough to submit. Although I do not have all of the answers, I do know Who to call on. God does have the answers.

There is nothing as terrible as sleeping beside someone you have not spoken to in three days. I was guilty of this before Justin and I were married. When I was angry with him, in order not to say the wrong thing, I just didn't say anything, and I later regretted it. After we were married, Justin and I agreed never to go to bed angry with each other (see Ephesians 4:26). From time to time, it did happen, but we never went a whole day without speaking to each other.

Chapter 10

Till Death Us Do Part

Jesus said to her, "I am the Resurrection and the Life. Whoever believes in (adheres to, trusts in, relies on) Me [as Savior] will live even if he dies; and everyone who lives and believes in Me [as Savior] will never die.   John 11:15-26

I know that throughout this testimony, it must seem as if Justin was a harsh or even a mean person. Believe me, he wasn't. My husband was very pleasant when he wasn't under the influence of drugs or alcohol. Our only arguments were about his mishandling of money or cheating on me with other women.

After a while I got used to him not coming home, so that was no longer an issue. I did what I could to ensure that our house was a great place for him to come home to. Our children were always taken care of, and I always had a healthy meal prepared. I prayed and asked God to enable me to be a pleasant wife to come home to, and I truly believe the Lord answered that prayer.

Still, even though I worked at being the best wife I could be, I began to notice a bit more of a struggle in Justin. I asked the Lord to allow me to see what I needed to see in order to help him. He was battling something spiritually that I didn't understand.

I grew angry with the devil, but this caused me to be upset with my husband's actions. He was still choosing the world's way (partying, staying away from home, and being with the wrong crowd) and not God's way. So, instead of me arguing with him about it, I would reveal to him naturally what the Lord was showing me spiritually. I would tell him what God was showing me about his friends, and then he would see that it was true. Still, he chose his own way.

I refused to allow any of this to throw me off course. I knew the enemy would try to get the best of me. So I continued to attend church regularly, bringing my children with me, and always extending an invitation to my husband. I desperately wanted to see his change come.

Soon our third-year anniversary came around, and I thought, "Okay, maybe we've just been doing the same routine too long," so I set out to get our little family on a couple of trips. I was sure that things would be different if I could get Justin away from home and away from his friends. I was sure that this would enable us to grow closer. At the moment, we were about as far apart as we had ever been.

But instead of enjoying these trips, Justin resented my dragging him away from home when what he wanted was to be with his circle of friends. I was made to feel bad for even thinking of taking the family on vacation. I kept praying.

I did not like who Justin had become. I could no longer recognize the man I had married. The world had changed him, and I began to understand that the enemy had a terrible stronghold on his life. I cried many nights, asking God to send Justin a man of God who could relate to his past troubles and help him overcome his current situation.

Justin still had recurring nightmares about the day he was shot by police and was being tormented in other ways. Occasionally he would confide in me about what he was going through. He was having dreams that the devil was holding him down and not letting him go or that he was running and reaching a door that he then could not open to get away from some demonic force that was chasing him.

These confessions had me wondering and praying about how I could help Justin. All I knew to do was take everything to the Lord in prayer.

One night the two of us got on our knees together, and I prayed for God to help him. I led him in a prayer of salvation, and then I trusted the Lord to do the rest. This was encouraging, but my spirit was not yet at peace because Justin continued to do the same things.

When September came, it was time for me to go to our annual women's retreat. I left Ha'Ryon with my sister Andrea, and I left Judah at home with his father. I figured Ha'Ryon would like to spend time with her cousins, and this would give Justin and Judah some bonding time, while I sought the Lord on behalf of the whole family.

I was tired (literally) and spiritually worn out. I felt as if I had been doing a whole lot of praying, and I needed more results. I almost changed my mind about going to the spiritual encounter, but I knew that the Holy Spirit was prompting me to push through my weariness and get there. Sometimes we don't feel like going or praying or praising, but I have learned that we must do it anyway.

The retreat began on a Friday and was set to end on a Sunday. I had procrastinated so long that I didn't get there until Saturday. God, however, was just waiting for me to get there because He had a word for me, and that word contained special instructions.

I praised and worshipped that day along with forty other women who were there also seeking God. Together we ushered the Holy Spirit into the room. It was such a warm and pleasant feeling, one that I had been longing for.

There were five ministers that weekend scheduled to preach, but one of them had gotten her dates all mixed up and almost didn't make it. I felt as if the enemy hadn't wanted me to receive that word from God, for the Holy Spirit spoke through this woman, calling me out of a crowd and speaking amazing things into my life. I felt as if the Lord Himself was telling me how I was to attract greatness to my life.

The Holy Spirit instructed me to pray for the next seven days for fifteen minutes a day and to tell the Lord my deepest desires. Then the Spirit said through her, "But there's just one more hurt." I began to sob, as the Lord re-leased the prophet to speak into my life. She said this hurt would be worse than any other, and I could sense that what she was saying was real.

When she had finished speaking to me, I went off into a corner and began to pray. I felt as if God had really laid a brick on my heart. I asked Him to help me and give me strength for whatever it was He would allow to happen next in my life.

When the weekend meeting was over, I went home with my head held high, but there were some definite questions still in my mind. Most of all, I wanted to know what this *hurt* would be. And I would still have to go before the Lord for the next seven days and tell Him my deepest desires. What should I tell Him?

I kept racking my brain, trying to figure out what could possibly hurt me more than I had already been hurt. At the same time, in my daily encounters, I began asking God for some material things. After the third day of telling God that my deepest desire was for a new home, I had to stop and realize that what God was talking about was something bigger than a new home. My prayer then changed and become, "Lord, my deepest desire is You."

For the last four days, I would get into the shower and call on the Holy Spirit, and He would meet me right there. I would began to weep, daily telling the Lord how I didn't want anything for my life that He didn't want.

God began to reveal to me things that Justin had been battling with for years that I'd had no knowledge of. He had a habit of keeping his lifestyle a secret from me and only telling me what he wanted me to know. Now the Lord opened a way into all of that secrecy.

The Lord not only showed me Justin's private lifestyle; He also showed me that Justin had been going through a deep depression, trying to deal with his past and some generational curses, and was worried about getting into legal trouble and possibly facing jail time (due to that police chase that got him shot). I realized that this situation was way bigger than me.

Then, somehow I suddenly knew what the *hurt* was that the Holy Spirit had spoken about, and all I could do was to pray, "Lord, please don't let Justin die in his sins." The words the Lord had spoken to me during the spiritual encounter had followed me ever since, and I had been praying for Justin more and more.

But now I began to fast and pray and to lay hands on him.

To tell you the truth, I was afraid of this *hurt* that was to come. God had never spoken to me in this way before, and I was unsure of just what was ahead of me. What I did know was that the Lord was preparing me for whatever was to come.

Almost two weeks before the Thanksgiving holidays, one of Justin's friends called him and informed him that another so-called friend had threatened his (Justin's) life. This was so far from anything I normally encountered in life. I knew the God I served, and yet I was still afraid, and so was Justin.

We quickly gathered up some things and left the house, afraid that someone would come and do us and our children harm. I prayed and prayed, while trying to make Justin see what his lifestyle had caused. I didn't put him down or make him feel less of a man, but as you can imagine, this situation had him more depressed than ever.

We only stayed away from home for one night, and when we went back to the house, nothing happened. We were all still safe for the moment.

That day I told Justin what the prophet had spoken to me and proceeded to ask him what his favorite color and flower were.

I do believe that God doesn't leave us in the dark about things. I felt as if something was about to happen to my husband. I didn't know what, but I did know that it would confirm what the Holy Spirit had spoken to me.

As Thanksgiving week approached, I was glad to have Justin around, but he was not the same. He seemed to be still afraid and had a lot on his mind. That Monday he made up his mind to get professional help in dealing with his depression. Personally, I'd had no idea that his state of depression had gotten so bad.

I didn't give up on Justin and never planned to, because I knew that if I gave up, then the enemy would have his way with him. Instead of giving up, I sought God more, and He gave me power in the midst of my hurt and pain so that I could stand in the gap and intercede for my husband.

Thanksgiving day came, and I remember whispering in Justin's ear, "With all we've been through, you have to give me at least thirty good years of marriage."

He responded, "We're going to live longer than that."

I was a bit relieved by that, but I was still unaware of the fact that Justin had a lot more on his mind than he was telling me, a lot more than I could ever have imagined. We had spoken about going to church together on Sunday, and I was happy that he had agreed.

When Sunday morning came, however, Justin was not home. He had stayed away from home all night. I was worried about him, but then he came home, so

I felt better. But I noticed that he had been drinking, and so he was unable to go with me to church that day.

Of course this frustrated me, but I thought, "Oh well, I'll go praise the Lord on his behalf." I could be assured, at least, that he was safe inside, lying on the sofa to get some rest and recover while I and the children were at church.

I walked out of the house, but he called me back inside for a kiss. I kissed him and told him I loved him, and then I went on to church.

I recall feeling a little empty as I arrived at the church, and then the Lord sent yet another spiritual covering for my life. I call her my Sister Terry.

Sister Terry said the Lord had sent her after me and, from what I could see, she was obedient to the Holy Spirit. She first informed me that I looked spaced out. I didn't know what to say to this.

Then she asked me to type into her phone what I wanted God to do for me. I proceeded to type: "I want God to heal

my husband, set him free from all bond-
ages and deliver him."

As I was doing this, she went to get
someone else to come pray with me. We
prayed together.

During the praise and worship that
morning, I lifted my hands, and it felt
as if an angel had literally wrapped its
wings around me and clothed me in
peace.

After the service was over and I pulled
up the driveway of our home, the Holy
Spirit spoke to me to leave the children
in the car. I wasn't sure what this meant
or why, but I knew what I felt, and so I
didn't question the Holy Spirit.

I calmly instructed the children to
wait in the car for a minute, assuring
them that I would be back soon. I'm
sure many will not understand this, but
you have to know how the Holy Spirit
works.

I went inside to check on Justin and
found him in exactly the same position
he had been in when I left. But when I

spoke to him, there was no response. His fingers were gray and cold, and so were his lips. It didn't take long for me to realized that my beloved husband had passed away in my absence.

My heart sank, but this was offset by the touch I had received from that angel at church. The angel seemed to be still with me, and a strange peace somehow overshadowed my sudden loss.

After attempting to revive Justin with CPR, I called 911 to report his non-responsiveness. Next I called his mom and told her what had happened. Then I called my mom and asked her if she could come and take the children so that I could be free to make any necessary arrangements.

It didn't dawn on me that day, but later I came to realize that this was the *hurt* God had spoken to me about. There was no way I could be angry with God, because He had been preparing me for this moment.

Yes, the hurt went very deep. It had never occurred to me that I would have to bury my husband. The only way I got through the funeral and burial was to sing to the Lord. As heavy as the atmosphere was, I felt a cloud of peace hovering over me the whole time. My husband was gone, but no one could take this peace from my soul.

Chapter 11

The New Birth

*For I know the plans and thoughts that I
have for you,' says the Lord, 'plans for peace
and well-being and not for disaster to give
you a future and a hope.* Jeremiah 29:11

I have repeated my original Bible text
here from Chapter 1, because this event
brought me full circle, and I found that
God had not changed His intent for my
life.

As you can imagine, that writing that
last chapter was very hard for me. I had
grown to trust the Lord so much, and
now I had suddenly lost my best friend.

I was determined not to give up on God. I would always trust Him, and I would always trust His Word, for it is true and never fails.

If I not been so spiritually prepared for this moment, I might have gone through trials that I didn't need to go through (for example, conflicts with family members). It didn't happen.

I found the grieving process to be highly emotional, and I learned that not everyone grieves in the same way. For my part, I was hurting. For one thing, Justin was the only man I could see myself with, so my future was uncertain.

In the midst of my own pain, I choose to take the power God had given me and pray for more strength to get through so that I could help others with their marriages. I felt as though I had passed an important test in life. I could have given up many times, but I chose to stick it out and win.

I was wondering what might have happened if I had given up and run away from my marriage, and the Holy Spirit spoke to me and said, "Because you have chosen to stay, I'll give you a testimony." So here it is ... my very own testimony.

Now you can say that you have read my story. Before you finish, allow me to ask you a question: what have you gotten from this? Can you say now that you want the Holy Spirit to show you things and speak to you too? Can you say, "I want to be closer to the Lord?" I can tell you that my strength has come from Him. In this world we live in today, we all need to be drawn closer to God.

Here's another question to ask yourself: "How do I become a better husband (or wife) so the Lord can be pleased with my marriage?" Your answer is simple: Christ. He is the only One who can save you, heal you, help you, deliver you, shape and mold you into who He desires you to be.

But you must first surrender to Him, giving up your own way. That sounds difficult, but I can testify that when I surrendered my life to Christ, it was not a hard thing for me to do. Now I had no will, and I had no way, but I knew that God was my heavenly Father, and that was all that mattered. He would be with me in the days ahead, would reveal each step I was to take and would help me to take it. I was at peace. I had learned *The Power of a Hurting Wife.*

My friend, now that you have read my story, I pray that you have developed a hunger and thirst to know the Lord like never before. I also pray that this is also not something you will take lightly because your future is at stake. The enemy doesn't want to see your marriage prosper, and if you are unhappy in your marriage and have been for quite some time, then I suggest that you ask yourself the question: "What position does God have in my marriage?" Let me inform you that He must be first in everything that we do.

I have added a prayer of salvation here at the end, and I trust that you will pray it from your heart, having faith to believe that God hears you and will answer you. Listen now for His answer.

A Prayer for Salvation

Lord, I open my heart to You, and I ask for Your forgiveness for all the sins I have committed. Cleanse me, Lord, and purge me from the filth of this world. Take away anything that is in me, Lord, that is not like You.

Lord, help me to understand that my life is not my own, and give me the direction I need to go in the way You want me to go. Draw near to me, O God, and help me draw near to You.

Give me wisdom, strength and knowledge where it's needed in my life and the desire to live by Your law. I love You, Lord, but please help me believe where I do not believe.

I surrender to You, Lord, my will for Your will. Send Your Holy Spirit to lead me, guide me and order my footsteps.

In Jesus' name
Amen!

The 30-Day Challenge

It has been said that it takes 28 days to develop any habit, whether bad or good. Accordingly, I created a challenge (with two extra days added on) that I believe can help you improve your marriage. I developed this challenge while going through a very rough time in my own marriage, so I know that it works.

The challenge simply consists of each spouse thinking of five things their mate could do to make the marriage better and then writing these down, exchanging papers and committing to try to work these issues out one by one.

Just to be safe, give yourself six weeks to take this challenge. You will begin the first week focusing on the first item on the list. From Monday through Friday, each spouse should do their best to meet the need and the required actions of their mates's number one item. Then, over the weekend, you, as a couple, should come together and take time to discuss week one, how it went, and how you might improve on it during the coming week. Pray together about it and share scriptural promises concerning it.

During week two, which should begin on the following Monday, you will continue to work on the first item in the list, attempting to do even better than you did the first week, but you will also start working on the second thing your spouse has written you could do to make your marriage work better.

Do the same with weeks three, four and five, each time adding a new item of endeavor, but also continuing to fulfill the previous weeks' items.

By week six, with enough prayer, all of the five items should be getting easier to accomplish and should be becoming a habit that you will continue doing to make life better for everyone concerned. I am not a marriage counselor, but this is something that I tried, and it worked for me.

Note: Both parties must be in agreement for this challenge to work. No one can be forced to do take such a challenge and expect good results.

A Self-Questionnaire

- Have you accepted Jesus Christ as your Lord and Savior?

  _____

- Where Does God stand in your life? Is He 1st? 2nd? 3rd? Or do you even know?

  _____

- Do you want a closer relationship with God? If so, what are you willing to give up to achieve it?

  _____

- Have you had enough of doing things your own way and have them not work out for you?

  _____

- Can you see yourself giving up all of your own ways and submitting all to the ways of God?

  _____

These are all good questions to ask yourself when seeking to have a closer and more intimate relationship with God and your spouse. Imagine praying to a God whom you only "know of" but do not really have a relationship with. That would be like a total stranger asking to have some of your personal property. You don't have a relationship with them so you are uncomfortable giving your things away to them.

God's Word tells us that if we confess with our mouths and believe in our hearts that Jesus Christ died on the cross for us, our sins will be forgiven (see Romans 10:9-10). It also tells us to seek first the Kingdom of God (see Matthew 6:33). This means that God should always be first in our thoughts, first in our day, first in our every decision, first even in our finances.

Putting God first also requires some sacrifices on our part, as far as the company we keep, the places we go and the things we say and do. As believers in Christ, our lives should model righteous living, and we should be so transparent that the world can look at us and see that God is living in us. A commitment to live a righteous life makes it easier for us to do things God's way, for we no longer have to make decisions on our own. Instead, the Holy Spirit becomes your Guide in all things.

I pray that will help you to get into God's Word and live a better life in Christ, while continuously drawing nearer to God.

Author Contact Page

If this book has been a blessing, you may contact the author directly in the following ways:

Allison Davis
720 N Joe Wilson Road
Cedar Hill, TX 75104

email: powerofahurtingwife@gmail.com
chinyeres.llc@gmail.com

Living

Out

the

Gospel

McDougal & Associates
*Servants of Christ and Stewards of the
Mysteries of God*